A Ghost Wandering Through a Memory

A DIFFERENT KIND OF READING OF "THE LOVE SONG OF J. ALFRED PRUFROCK"

BY

PETER DAMIAN BELLIS

River Boat Books

A Ghost Wandering Through a Memory: A Different Kind of Reading of "The Love Song of J. Alfred Prufrock"
Copyright © 2021 by Peter Damian Bellis

The poem "The Love Song of J. Alfred Prufrock" by T. S. Eliot reprinted in this volume is in the Public Domain.

Cover artwork adapted from the painting titled *Lido* by Max Beckmann, 1924. Used under the "Fair Use" provision of U. S. Copyright law.

First River Boat Books printing: September 22, 2021.
Second edition (revised) February 15, 2025.
ISBN: 978-1-955823-05-0

Literary Criticism. Poetry.

"The truth is not that we need the critics in order to enjoy the authors, but that we need the authors in order to enjoy the critics."
—C. S. Lewis

A Ghost Wandering Through a Memory

A DIFFERENT KIND OF READING OF
"THE LOVE SONG OF J. ALFRED PRUFROCK"

CONTENTS

"THE LOVE SONG OF J. ALFRED PRUFROCK" —9
BY T.S. ELIOT

A GHOST WANDERING THROUGH A MEMORY: A —15
DIFFERENT KIND OF READING OF "THE LOVE
SONG OF J. ALFRED PRUFROCK"
BY PETER DAMIAN BELLIS

> A SHORT DIGRESSION ON OTHER CRITICAL —19
> VIEWPOINTS WITH RESPECT TO THE CHARACTER
> PRUFROCK:

> THE BEGINNING OF THE TALE, THE BEGINNING OF —21
> THE JOURNEY:

> A SHORT DIGRESSION ON THOSE CRITICS WHO —29
> SUGGEST THAT ELIOT'S LITANY OF "THERE WILL BE
> TIME" IS ALLUDING EITHER TO ANDREW MARVEL'S
> "TO HIS COY MISTRESS" OR TO ECCLESIASTES 3:1-8
> OR TO BOTH:

> BACK TO THE UNFOLDING SCENE: —32

> GOING BEYOND THE TAKING OF A TEA: —39

> UNDERSTANDING JUST WHAT THE OVERWHELMING —41
> QUESTION ACTUALLY IS:

DIGRESSION ON DIFFERENCES BETWEEN THE FIRST DRAFT OF PRUFROCK AND ITS FINAL FORM AS IT RELATES TO BOTH THE OVERWHELMING QUESTION AND THE CHARACTER OF PRUFROCK:	—44
BACK TO THE UNFOLDING SCENE ONE MORE TIME:	—48
WOULD ACTING DIFFERENTLY HAVE MATTERED?:	—51
THE MEANING OF THE *HAMLET* STANZA	—58
THE LAST FEW SCENES OF THE MOVIE OF PRUFROCK'S LIFE AND THE END OF THE POEM:	—61

The Love Song of J. Alfred Prufrock
(by T.S. Eliot)

> *S'io credesse che mia risposta fosse*
> *A persona che mai tornasse al mondo,*
> *Questa fiamma staria senza piu scosse.*
> *Ma percioche giammai di questo fondo*
> *Non torno vivo alcun, s'i'odo il vero,*
> *Senza tema d'infamia ti rispondo.*

Let us go then, you and I,
When the evening is spread out against the sky
Like a patient etherized upon a table;
Let us go, through certain half-deserted streets,
The muttering retreats
Of restless nights in one-night cheap hotels
And sawdust restaurants with oyster-shells:
Streets that follow like a tedious argument
Of insidious intent
To lead you to an overwhelming question ...
Oh, do not ask, "What is it?"
Let us go and make our visit.

In the room the women come and go
Talking of Michelangelo.

The yellow fog that rubs its back upon the window-panes,
The yellow smoke that rubs its muzzle on the window-panes,
Licked its tongue into the corners of the evening,

Lingered upon the pools that stand in drains,
Let fall upon its back the soot that falls from
    chimneys,
Slipped by the terrace, made a sudden leap,
And seeing that it was a soft October night,
Curled once about the house, and fell asleep.

And indeed there will be time
For the yellow smoke that slides along the street,
Rubbing its back upon the window-panes;
There will be time, there will be time
To prepare a face to meet the faces that you meet;
There will be time to murder and create,
And time for all the works and days of hands
That lift and drop a question on your plate;
Time for you and time for me,
And time yet for a hundred indecisions,
And for a hundred visions and revisions,
Before the taking of a toast and tea.

In the room the women come and go
Talking of Michelangelo.

And indeed there will be time
To wonder, "Do I dare?" and, "Do I dare?"
Time to turn back and descend the stair,
With a bald spot in the middle of my hair —
(They will say: "How his hair is growing thin!")
My morning coat, my collar mounting firmly to
    the chin,
My necktie rich and modest, but asserted by a
    simple pin —

A Ghost Wandering Through a Memory

(They will say: "But how his arms and legs are
    thin!")
Do I dare   45
Disturb the universe?
In a minute there is time
For decisions and revisions which a minute will
    reverse.

For I have known them all already, known them
    all:
Have known the evenings, mornings, afternoons,   50
I have measured out my life with coffee spoons;
I know the voices dying with a dying fall
Beneath the music from a farther room.
        So how should I presume?

And I have known the eyes already, known them
    all—   55
The eyes that fix you in a formulated phrase,
And when I am formulated, sprawling on a pin,
When I am pinned and wriggling on the wall,
Then how should I begin
To spit out all the butt-ends of my days and ways? 60
        And how should I presume?

And I have known the arms already, known them
    all—
Arms that are braceleted and white and bare
(But in the lamplight, downed with light brown
    hair!)
Is it perfume from a dress   65
That makes me so digress?

Arms that lie along a table, or wrap about a shawl.
    And should I then presume?
    And how should I begin?

Shall I say, I have gone at dusk through narrow
    streets   70
And watched the smoke that rises from the pipes
Of lonely men in shirt-sleeves, leaning out of
    windows? ...

I should have been a pair of ragged claws
Scuttling across the floors of silent seas.

And the afternoon, the evening, sleeps so
    peacefully!   75
Smoothed by long fingers,
Asleep ... tired ... or it malingers,
Stretched on the floor, here beside you and me.
Should I, after tea and cakes and ices,
Have the strength to force the moment to its crisis? 80
But though I have wept and fasted, wept and
    prayed,
Though I have seen my head (grown slightly bald)
    brought in upon a platter,
I am no prophet — and here's no great matter;
I have seen the moment of my greatness flicker,
And I have seen the eternal Footman hold my coat, 85
    and snicker,
And in short, I was afraid.

And would it have been worth it, after all,
After the cups, the marmalade, the tea,

A Ghost Wandering Through a Memory

Among the porcelain, among some talk of you and
   me,
Would it have been worth while, 90
To have bitten off the matter with a smile,
To have squeezed the universe into a ball
To roll it towards some overwhelming question,
To say: "I am Lazarus, come from the dead,
Come back to tell you all, I shall tell you all"— 95
If one, settling a pillow by her head
      Should say: "That is not what I meant at all;
      That is not it, at all."

And would it have been worth it, after all,
Would it have been worth while, 100
After the sunsets and the dooryards and the
   sprinkled streets,
After the novels, after the teacups, after the skirts
   that trail along the floor—
And this, and so much more?—
It is impossible to say just what I mean!
But as if a magic lantern threw the nerves in
   patterns on a screen: 105
Would it have been worth while
If one, settling a pillow or throwing off a shawl,
And turning toward the window, should say:
      "That is not it at all,
      That is not what I meant, at all." 110

No! I am not Prince Hamlet, nor was meant to be;
Am an attendant lord, one that will do
To swell a progress, start a scene or two,
Advise the prince; no doubt, an easy tool,

Deferential, glad to be of use, 115
Politic, cautious, and meticulous;
Full of high sentence, but a bit obtuse;
At times, indeed, almost ridiculous—
Almost, at times, the Fool.

I grow old ... I grow old ... 120
I shall wear the bottoms of my trousers rolled.

Shall I part my hair behind?   Do I dare to eat a peach?
I shall wear white flannel trousers, and walk upon the beach.
I have heard the mermaids singing, each to each.

I do not think that they will sing to me. 125

I have seen them riding seaward on the waves
Combing the white hair of the waves blown back
When the wind blows the water white and black.

We have lingered in the chambers of the sea
By sea-girls wreathed with seaweed red and brown 130
Till human voices wake us, and we drown.

A Ghost Wandering Through a Memory –
A DIFFERENT KIND OF READING OF
"THE LOVE SONG OF J. ALFRED PRUFROCK"
(by Peter Damian Bellis)

"If I thought that my reply were given to anyone who might return to the world, this flame would stand forever still; but since never from this deep place has anyone returned alive, if what I hear is true, without fear of infamy I answer thee."

Eliot's poem "Prufrock" begins with this quote, which is from Dante's *Inferno* at the point when the soul of Guido Montefelatro speaks to a pilgrim who has asked Guido to tell his story. Guido Montefelatro was a devious general who battled against the forces of Pope Martin IV from 1282 through 1283 but later accepted the authority of Pope Honorius IV in 1286. He was excommunicated by Pope Nicholas III in 1288 and then had this excommunication rescinded in 1296 for helping Pope Boniface VIII battle his enemies. In 1296 Guido became a Franciscan monk, and it is this changing of his colors, so to speak, that Dante condemns in *Inferno*. Dante put Guido in Hell in the ring of the Fraudulent because Guido was no longer true to himself. (More about this point later, because this is precisely what the overwhelming question in "Prufrock" is all about.)

So what is happening with this quote from

Dante? Why is Eliot quoting these lines in such prominent fashion? Is he drawing an implicit parallel between Prufrock and Guido? Yes, he is. Not in terms of the specifics of Guido's life and the sins he committed on the battlefield; warfare and battles are not a part of Prufrock's tale. But "yes" in terms of how each character functions within the literary world they inhabit.

Point one: the use of these lines from Dante sets the stage and lets us know what kind of story to expect as the poem unfolds. We will experience a Dantesque story. In a "Talk on Dante" (T. S. Eliot, *The Kenyon Review*, Vol. 14, No. 2, The Dante Number (Spring, 1952), pp. 178-188), Eliot says "Certainly I have borrowed lines from him [Dante], in the attempt to reproduce, or rather arouse in the reader's mind the memory of some Dantesque scene...." So Eliot is trying to set up a Dantesque atmosphere in "Prufrock"; the landscape in Eliot's poem is an updated version of Dante's landscape in *Inferno*. In other words, the literary world each character inhabits can be defined as a type of Hell. Guido inhabits a Hell characterized by a sense of isolation. His Hell does not cause him physical suffering, but it causes him intense mental anguish, so the chance to tell his tale to a pilgrim is in fact a welcome opportunity to escape his Hell, if only for the time it takes to share his story. Prufrock's Hell is perhaps more personalized, like the Hell presented in Sartre's *No*

A Ghost Wandering Through a Memory

Exit; it is a product of his personal choices in life, and, as is the case with Guido, it does not cause him any physical suffering, but he is tormented to some degree by the fact that he is now in Hell. The poem then is a working out of what is bothering Prufrock. But it is the lines from Dante at the beginning of "Prufrock" that provide the clue as to what is happening here; these lines provide the lens through which to see the poem, to see what happens and why, and to find meaning.

Point two: we are meant to see and understand the character Prufrock through the lens of Dante. Of course that begs a question, and this question is directed at the critics over the years who have interpreted (or misinterpreted) "Prufrock." Why do we not take Eliot at his word in terms of the nature of the parallel he is drawing between Guido and Prufrock? Guido is in Hell. He will share his story with a pilgrim. Prufrock is in Hell. He will share his story with a pilgrim (the you of the first line). Guido can never return to the world above; he is dead, his story will remain in Hell. But here the parallel for most critics seems to come to an abrupt halt, for they all read the poem as if Prufrock is alive; some even read it as if the poem is about squandered second chances. But if Guido is dead, which he is, then Prufrock must also be dead; he must also, like Guido, be trapped in a personalized Hell, waiting for a pilgrim to come along so he can share his tale. For both tell a tale, which also means that we, the reader of "Prufrock" (the poem), are also the pilgrim in the poem.

Thinking of Prufrock as dead from the beginning of the poem, a shade come back to take us on a journey (for Prufrock's way of sharing his tale is to take us on a journey through his memories, rather like the ghost of Christmas Past takes Scrooge on a similar journey) is a rather simple and straight-forward way of viewing the poem. It is also liberating, for it changes the way you read many of the lines, and provides a rather compelling framework for integrating all aspects of the poem. Of course this is not a normal recounting of a tale. This is a tale told by reliving it, by wandering through the memory of it, a dream-like wandering, lingering here, there, moving forward and backward in time, stretching time and space, compressing time and space, and inviting the reader (the pilgrim) to participate in this strange journey. It is a tale told by a ghost, who tells it because he, like Guido in Dante, no longer fears any recriminations from those who were a part of the tale, for he is now beyond their reach, a fact which becomes clear by the end of the poem.

A SHORT DIGRESSION ON OTHER CRITICAL VIEWPOINTS WITH RESPECT TO THE CHARACTER PRUFROCK:

Just a quick word about those critics who assume Prufrock is alive. Grover Cleveland Smith asserts that Prufrock is a Henry James type character; moreover, he says that Eliot specifically used a Henry James story, "Crapy Cornelia," as a model for Prufrock. Smith writes "In the middle-class would-be suitor White-Mason of 'Crapy Cornelia,' Eliot found a character endowed with certain pretensions to cultivation or dignity... ." And later, Smith states "besides manifesting a Jamesian type, Prufrock seems to regard himself in a Jamesian light. Unlike other sentimental bachelors, from Charles Lamb's to Ilk Marvel's, he introspects to break his way out, not wholly unsuccessfully. For at least he achieves a rhetoric of mythic grandeur . . . (p. 153, *T.S. Eliot and the Use of Memory*)"

The issue I have with Mr. Smith's assertion is that it comes from outside the poem. The label "Jamesian" comes from Smith, not Eliot. And while Eliot may very well have modeled Prufrock after the characters he encountered in James' stories, there is nothing here to link the Prufrock character specifically to White-Mason. Smith and other critics will point out that the story of "Crapy Cornelia" is similar to the story in "Prufrock."

They will say "look here, White-Mason, the hero of 'Crapy Cornelia,' returns home after being abroad, is about to propose marriage to Mrs. Worthington but is distracted by Cornelia Rasch, a friend from earlier days, so the proposal never takes place." I will only say to such critics: the whole idea that Prufrock is seeking to propose to one of the women in the poem does not come from within the poem either; this notion also comes from outside the poem, and so it is manifestly, or one might say absurdly false. More about that last point later.

This kind of interpretation is based on a false premise, for it assumes as a truth that Eliot's Prufrock was based on a specific character in another story, a character who was unable to deliver a marriage proposal, and then it uses that assumption to assert that the action in Prufrock must be the same as in the story where that other character exists. It is an example of circular reasoning as well because from there it is quite easy to use the invented fact that Prufrock is unable to deliver this marriage proposal as proof that he is a Jamesian type character. Yet neither assumption is provable if you stay within the confines of the poem itself.

My suggestion here with respect to "Crapy Cornelia" is that we cannot properly call it an allusion within the poem, so we need not worry about connecting the meaning of that particular short story to the meaning of Prufrock.

THE BEGINNING OF THE TALE, THE BEGINNING OF THE JOURNEY:

    Let us take the lines from Dante as a starting point. Let us further begin quite literally with the idea that Prufrock has lived his life, has been judged by his maker and is now serving out his sentence in what for him is a kind of Hell. A pilgrim arrives and wishes to hear Prufrock's tale. Prufrock is happy to oblige:

    LET us go then, you and I,

    But since it is a tale that must be experienced, they head out into a landscape that has a visceral albeit dream-like reality. Perhaps this landscape is a vision of Prufrock's past, the life he once lived, but it is most certainly a vision of his present torment, his personal Hell. It is a world in a comatose state:

    When the evening is spread out against the sky
    Like a patient etherized upon a table;

This world is as empty as a ghost town with "half-deserted streets" and, at least as far as we can tell, a single ghost – Prufrock. Further, these streets are defined or described as:

    The muttering retreats   5
    Of restless nights in one-night cheap hotels
    And sawdust restaurants with oyster-shells:

Why muttering? The word suggests a constant but personal condemnation of the circumstance that might cause such muttering – i.e. a life spent in cheap, dingy surroundings, a life marked by impermanence and inevitable decline (sawdust not trees or wood; oyster shells, not the oysters), a world in keeping with the image of a ghost town.

But the streets serve another function in the poem beyond merely a description of the world that Prufrock must journey through on his way to tell his tale. These streets are:

> Streets that follow like a tedious argument
> Of insidious intent
> To lead you to an overwhelming question....   10

In other words, these streets are reminders for Prufrock of a question he once faced because they force him to confront this question. We do not truly know if Prufrock once lived in these streets or is now condemned to live in them; but we do not need to know. That question would perhaps lead us down a dead end (pun intended). Perhaps a better question to ask is: what purpose do the streets serve in this poem, a poem which, as the opening lines from Dante suggest, is also quite literally the visible rendering of wandering through a Dantesque landscape.

One gets the feeling that Prufrock knows he will face this overwhelming question because that is where the streets lead. Moreover, one also gets

A Ghost Wandering Through a Memory

the feeling that Prufrock has taken this journey before because the journey through the streets is characterized as a "tedious argument," one that he has heard before or perhaps made himself, and this argument is of "insidious intent," meaning it works on Prufrock's mind in sly, cunning fashion, without any conscious effort on Prufrock's part. It is rather like the moment when you hear a song on the radio and unbidden a memory pops into your mind. In Prufrock's case, all he needs to do to face the overwhelming question is take the journey. In fact just the mere mention of taking this journey sets his mind in motion.

Of course we, the reader and the pilgrim of the poem, the "you" who accompanies Prufrock, are curious about the question. But Prufrock puts us off.

> Oh, do not ask, "What is it?"
> Let us go and make our visit.

So we embark on our journey and immediately we are confronted with another new reality.

> In the room the women come and go
> Talking of Michelangelo.

Where did the women come from? And what is this room all of a sudden? Since we are no longer in the streets, we can infer that this new place is where we will face the overwhelming question.

Prufrock already told us as much. And since we are wandering through a dream landscape, we should expect such spatial and even temporal shifts, because the laws of ordinary physics do not apply in a world that exists outside of time and space (and this is true whether that world is a supernatural world where ghosts live and take pilgrims on visits; or whether that world exists in the imagination, where ghosts who play hosts to pilgrims also dwell). But leaving aside the dramatic shift in scene, all I can think of is this: what have the women to do with the overwhelming question? And what does Michelangelo have to do with the scene?

Other critics seem to think that Prufrock is afraid of these women, that he cannot get up the courage to speak to them, that he wanted to ask them out for a date, or perhaps he wished to marry one of them but never popped the question, and that his vacillation in this matter, his lack of courage, is why he has descended into a world of despair. I certainly do not see all of that here in this couplet.

I see women talking about Michelangelo.

Moreover, the name Michelangelo is what stands out, both poetically (for the name is the concluding zinger of the couplet) and in terms of meaning (the same reason). The women do not stand out. Even though they are the subject of the sentence, which gives us the impression that they

A Ghost Wandering Through a Memory

are the focus of Prufrock's (Eliot's) thinking, they are overpowered by the presence of Michelangelo. So Michelangelo is the focus, not the women. And then I remember that Michelangelo's masterpiece *The Last Judgement* was inspired by Dante's *Divine Comedy*. So then I am thinking that this poem, this wandering through a dream landscape, is in part about Prufrock coming to terms with some judgement, and since the only judgement evident up to this point is that of Prufrock abiding in a quasi-Hell, it seems clear that the poem is about Prufrock coming to terms with his own fate. He must accept his own last judgement, a judgement that has put him where he is. And yes, it is clear that the overwhelming question is in some way connected to this sense that Prufrock must accept his judgement (of what? God? Time? Life? – maybe they are all the same thing).

Of course it is natural to wonder why the women are talking of Michelangelo in the first place. But it seems to me here that Eliot is simply setting a trap for us. Eliot does not reveal the depth of the women's discussion, which also suggests that perhaps there is no depth to it. We are left to measure the lingering echo of the importance of the name Michelangelo on our own.

With the next stanza, we are focused on the exterior landscape once again.

> The yellow fog that rubs its back upon the
>   window-panes,   15

> The yellow smoke that rubs its muzzle on the
> window-panes
> Licked its tongue into the corners of the
> evening,
> Lingered upon the pools that stand in drains,
> Let fall upon its back the soot that falls from
> chimneys,
> Slipped by the terrace, made a sudden leap,   20
> And seeing that it was a soft October night,
> Curled once about the house, and fell asleep.

Have we been outside the room all the while and were we only looking in through the window panes of the house, outside which we now stand? Or did we simply leave the room and appear outside the house that contains the room? I do not think the answer matters. I think the purpose of this stanza is to characterize the relationship between the room where the overwhelming question is faced, and the visual aspects of the Hell where Prufrock now resides as a result of whatever went on in that room. The yellow fog and yellow smoke suggest a Dantesque kind of Hell, but the overall imagery suggests a housecat curling up for the night, which suggests to me that Prufrock's journey through Hell is something of a comfortable ritual; in other words, a ritual that he has experienced again and again.

So let me characterize what is happening here dramatically. As if I were supplying the stage

A Ghost Wandering Through a Memory

directions, which are missing from the original poem.

Prufrock and the pilgrim embark on a journey to a room where an overwhelming question is to be faced. The moment the journey begins, we are in the room, or watching what takes place in the room. We see the women moving back and forth, talking of Michelangelo.

And then Prufrock **PAUSES** the scene.

The landscape that is a reflection of Prufrock's personal Hell settles in for the rest of the story. The landscape is not part of the story. It is the frame and boundary of the story and will assert itself once the story has concluded, as it always does. It is part of the ritual of telling/sharing the story.

In the next stanza, Prufrock is actually speaking to the pilgrim (the reader, the "you").

The scene that will unfold in the room **IS STILL PAUSED.**

The next action in the scene will be "the taking of a toast and tea." But between the women coming and going and the taking of the tea, we have Prufrock ruminating on the time between the two events and what might take place in the interval. Of course given that the scene is paused, there is much that could happen. Remember, we exist with Prufrock outside of time and space.

Prufrock begins his litany of what might happen in between the interval of unfolding events by acknowledging the landscape that is a reflection of his personal Hell.

> And indeed there will be time
> For the yellow smoke that slides along the
>   street,
> Rubbing its back upon the window panes;   25

He then asserts that there will be time to hide one's true self in preparation for social interaction in this interval in between.

> There will be time, there will be time
> To prepare a face to meet the faces that you
>   meet;

And the length of time that Prufrock imagines here seems to grow because the next task would require more time, more effort.

> There will be time to murder and create,

Is he only reflecting on possibilities; or is this litany related to the overwhelming question? Of course it is related to the question, though it is not yet clear just what that question is.

> And time for all the works and days of hands
> That lift and drop a question on your plate;   30

And now Prufrock turns to the pilgrim (the "you" the reader) and says:

> Time for you and time for me,
> And time yet for a hundred indecisions,
> And for a hundred visions and revisions,
> Before the taking of a toast and tea.

The movement of these possibilities seems to be a progression from the very specific task of getting ready to go to a party to exploring the infinite ("a hundred visions and revisions"), but all of it leads with some inevitability to the overwhelming question. Each possibility expands upon the previous possibility. But the very moment the possibility of infinite possibilities is suggested, Prufrock and we the reader are back at the beginning of the unfolding scene (line 35) watching the women come and go, and preparing ourselves for the question Prufrock will face.

A SHORT DIGRESSION ON THOSE CRITICS WHO SUGGEST THAT ELIOT'S LITANY OF "THERE WILL BE TIME" IS ALLUDING EITHER TO ANDREW MARVEL'S "TO HIS COY MISTRESS" OR TO ECCLESIASTES 3:1-8 OR TO BOTH:

A good many critics suggest that in the interval between the women coming and going and the taking of the tea, Eliot is alluding to Andrew Marvels' "To His Coy Mistress." They say that when Eliot writes: "There will be time ..." he is referring to Marvell's urging of his Mistress to seize the day in terms of an affair the two are having. The critics point to the very first line of Marvel's poem, which says: "Had we but world enough and time," and see, here it is, the allusion. Some of these critics even go so far as to suggest that Eliot is here using this allusion to poke fun at the romantic poets and at Prufrock by pointing out the irony that there will be time for Prufrock to try to express his feelings and then be rejected, not loved by a mistress. The problem with this line of reasoning is twofold. First, while Marvel is indeed addressing a woman in the first line of his poem, Prufrock is not addressing the women in his litany. None of the possibilities he raises are addressing a relationship with a woman (and here to say that the line referring to the overwhelming question is a reference to having a relationship with a woman is to be guilty of proving a thing by assuming the thing is true).

Secondly, the exhortation to continue an affair (Marvel) is quite the opposite from the marriage proposal that many critics say is the essence of the overwhelming question in Prufrock. Now one could argue that Prufrock is having an affair with one or more of these women, and then one could make a comparison to Marvel's poem. Indeed, it is clear from the poem itself that Prufrock did in fact have intimate relations with these women, for he says:

A Ghost Wandering Through a Memory

> I have known the arms already, known them all—
> Arms that are braceleted and white and bare
> (But in the lamplight, downed with light brown hair!)
> Is it perfume from a dress   65
> That makes me so digress?

In fact, one gets the impression that Prufrock was with these women in a very intimate setting, and in 1915, the year the poem was written, the kind of intimate scene described here was tantamount to having sex (similar to Hollywood movies from the 1940s and 1950s that would show a couple sitting on the corner of a bed and then in the next scene that same couple would be smoking cigarettes). When Prufrock says "Is it perfume from a dress/That makes me so digress," one gets the distinct impression that the women described above are no longer wearing their dresses, they are detached from their dress, which is also why he emphasizes that their arms are "white and bare." The fact that the scene takes place in lamplight is yet another detail that suggests this is a scene of intimacy. But if you are a critic suggesting that Prufrock is afraid of these women, it is problematic to then also assert he is having an affair with one or more of them. The bottom line here is that to say Eliot is alluding to any line in Marvel's "To His Coy Mistress" is a stretch at best, even the first line ("Had we but world enough, and time"), which is about more than having time anyway, so if Eliot was responding to this statement, his response is incomplete.

It is far more logical to suggest that Eliot is alluding to *Ecclesiastes* 3:1-8, for that passage is in fact a litany of all of the many things that may or will happen over time, but the passage in Ecclesiastes is about assigning the proper time for each and everything under the sun, while Prufrock's litany represents a very specific progression from a specific kind of response in a specific social setting to an infinity of possibilities, which suggests to me that Prufrock is imagining that anything can happen. In other words, there is no set time for anything that might happen. So I think it is also a bit of a stretch to say that Eliot means us to think of Ecclesiastes 3:1-8 while Prufrock is pondering what he might have done in the interval in between moments. Perhaps the litany is all just wishful thinking on Prufrock's part and nothing more.

BACK TO THE UNFOLDING SCENE:

So imagine you are standing there with Prufrock as he has paused the scene. His litany of what might take place in the interval in between moments is preparing us to properly appreciate

A Ghost Wandering Through a Memory

the scene that will unfold, a scene that will bring us face to face with the overwhelming question, as we are re-living a scene that once took place, a scene that seems to have taken place many times (many times while Prufrock was alive and many more times since he became a ghost).

One also gets the feeling that it is here that Prufrock wishes the outcome of the scene might have been different (the wished-for infinity of possibilities). It is as if he is saying 'here, yet, there is still time,' which is another way of saying my fate had not yet been decided at this point. I could have made a change, and thus a difference, at this point in the tale.

Then the couplet is repeated and we are back inside the room and the scene begins to unfold:

> In the room the women come and go   35
> Talking of Michelangelo.

And then Prufrock hits the **PAUSE** button yet again, and again, he begins to ruminate, but this time his ruminations are more specific, more personalized; it is as if he has entered the unfolding scene as both observer and actor (or he imagines that he has):

> And indeed there will be time
> To wonder, "Do I dare?" and, "Do I dare?"
> Time to turn back and descend the stair,
> With a bald spot in the middle of my hair— 40

> (They will say: "How his hair is growing thin!")
> My morning coat, my collar mounting firmly to the chin,
> My necktie rich and modest, but asserted by a simple pin—
> (They will say: "But how his arms and legs are thin!")

Again, Prufrock is asserting that here as we watch this moment, there is still time to change, to ask the question, to perhaps stand up for oneself in the face of petty comments. It also is clear that Prufrock chooses not to give the faceless people in this stanza the chance to utter the petty comments he imagines, which also robs him of the opportunity to respond to what these people would have or might have said. Now there are some critics who look at the above passage and assert that Prufrock is hesitant, afraid to assert himself, afraid to make changes, easily intimidated. This view seems to me to be contradicted both by elements within the poem, and by the very fact that Prufrock is dead and is no longer truly concerned with the reactions of others.

Consider his own self-deprecating remarks as proof of this assertion. He describes himself above as possessing "a bald spot in the middle" of his hair and suggests that the people he imagines will mock that. He imagines himself wearing a morning coat with his collar mounted "firmly to the chin," which means he is finely dressed, but the women only notice his thin arms and legs. Yet Prufrock himself mocks his baldness later on in the poem (line 82) when he says "Though I have seen my head (grown slightly bald) brought in upon a platter." The line is also wryly ironic, for as a head sans body, he has effectively rendered the imagined criticisms of the women—that his arms and legs are thin—a moot point. The ability to be self-deprecating in this manner seems inconsistent with being afraid of what others might say.

Finally, Prufrock is telling his tale in Hell and such tales do not escape the boundaries of Hell, a fact which is part of the meaning of the epigraph at the beginning of the poem.

So Prufrock does not seem to me to be hesitant or afraid. Rather he seems to be able to look himself directly in the eye and state honestly what he sees. In other words, he seems much more courageous than most critics assert.

Then Prufrock reflects upon what would happen (or what would have happened) if he acted (or had acted) differently.

Do I dare
Disturb the universe?

One could argue that Prufrock has all but entered the moment that is unfolding. In some ways it is like he is Scrooge trying to get his younger self to act differently. But does Eliot want us to believe that Prufrock could change the past? I think not. I think the question Prufrock poses here is more philosophical in nature; it is concerned with how we experience reality, how we experience time. It is also worth noting that Eliot thought a great deal about time. For example, the opening of his poem "Burnt Norton" (the first poem of Eliot's *Four Quartets)*, suggests that all time exists simultaneously. ("Time present and time past/Are both perhaps present in time future/ And time future contained in the past.") So here it seems that Eliot is giving voice to his own ruminations through the voice of Prufrock. Do I act differently, Prufrock seems to be saying, and so destroy the relationship between time and reality ("the universe")? But then he accepts that he can no longer make a change and immediately shifts the focus of his thoughts and reflects on how many opportunities he had to act differently.

> In a minute there is time
> For decisions and revisions which a minute
>   will reverse.

Is Prufrock here saying that he had only a minute to change his destiny? No! He is saying that in any minute there is time to change direction, or vacillate and not change direction. So while the scene we are witnessing is a fixed moment which we can comment upon, the implication is that there are also, or there were, many such moments in Prufrock's life. He had many moments when he could have changed direction. In fact given the ritualized nature of this journey we are on, it is impossible not to think that the scene played out with the women happened many times while Prufrock was alive. He says as much in the next stanza.

> For I have known them all already, known
>   them all:
> Have known the evenings, mornings, after-
>   noons,
> I have measured out my life with coffee
>   spoons;

He has known all of the moments when he could have changed direction. He has been careful in marking those moments (this is not so much a suggestion that he is timid, as some critics have suggested, but rather an indication that while alive he was conscious of the inner struggle to act differently, a struggle that still plagues him in death, for he is unable up till this point to accept the consequences of not acting differently).

But now we have a shift in the scene. Now we have Prufrock retreating from the unfolding scene and commenting on the present. In all likelihood, he is turning to the pilgrim as he says these lines.

> I know the voices dying with a dying fall

> Beneath the music from a farther room.
> So how should I presume?

In every other instance, both in the stanza that precedes this one and the one that follows, Prufrock is commenting on things known from the past. "I have known" he says. But here is the one instance when he says "I know" and puts the act of knowing in the present. He is speaking of his own death here "beneath the music" in a different room, not the room with the women talking of Michelangelo, "a farther room," the room where he now resides as a ghost. His death is the "dying fall," and as he was dying, the voices he heard around him, (perhaps the very human voices that "wake us" which he mentions at the end of the poem), these voices also die, meaning he is no longer able to hear them, which suggests that the concluding line here ("So how should I presume") refers to the act of thinking he could have made a change, that he could have acted differently while alive, or that even now he could act differently: both possibilities are precluded. To presume otherwise asks too much of Prufrock's imagination.

So what I see here is Prufrock the ghost, who has taken a pilgrim (the reader) to see/experience his story, now suddenly interjecting himself into this scene at this moment. It is similar to the kind of interjecting he did above when he suggested that there was still time to make a change at this point in the unfolding scene. The difference between the two moments is that during the "there will be time" litany, Prufrock's interjection was on a more abstract, theoretical level; but here, now, it seems that it could be an actual possibility, though, as noted above, Prufrock also seems to reject that possibility ("How should I presume") even as he considers it.

[Note: I am suddenly reminded of the play within a play structure that we see in *Hamlet*, for here, too, in Eliot's "Prufrock" we see a scene unfold, and that scene is contained within a larger scene unfolding. And the fact that in the climax of the poem (lines 111-119), Prufrock compares himself to both Hamlet and Polonius, seems to confirm that Eliot is making use of this kind of structure within a structure to highlight the degree to which his main character, like both Hamlet and Polonius, is a master of dissembling when it comes to getting at the truth about what is really happening.]

GOING BEYOND THE TAKING OF A TEA:

In lines 55-61, Prufrock returns to addressing various aspects of the unfolding scene, but since some of these aspects are not confined to the interval between the women coming and going and the taking of a tea, he must go outside the moment to other moments, generalized moments that provide a sense of how he lived his life and why he acted as he had.

> And I have known the eyes already, known them all— 55
> The eyes that fix you in a formulated phrase,

So not his true self, a caricature of his true self as seen by others, a false face as well that in all probability was a reflection of that face which he had prepared to meet other faces.

Then he comments on the action of the unfolding scene as if there are moments yet to come. He is most certainly motioning for the pilgrim to take a closer look at this scene.

> And when I am formulated, sprawling on a pin,
> When I am pinned and wriggling on the wall,

An image of how others saw him, a fixed image to last until the moment of his death and beyond (the image of a specimen on display comes to mind), for he did nothing to challenge this image while alive.

> Then how should I begin
> To spit out all the butt-ends of my days and ways? 60
> And how should I presume?

He is turning to the pilgrim as he says this. ("How should I [NOW] begin?") It is an implicit

A Ghost Wandering Through a Memory

acknowledgement that he was unable to "tell his tale" in life. It is also rather ironic, as he is *now* in death telling his tale (spitting "out the butt-ends of [his] days and ways") to the pilgrim; but again he is unable to share this tale with those in the unfolding scene, as much as he might wish to. His tale will not go beyond the boundaries of the Hell where he finds himself, just as Guido asserted that his tale would remain within those same boundaries.

UNDERSTANDING JUST WHAT THE OVERWHELMING QUESTION ACTUALLY IS:

As noted earlier, many critics assert that the overwhelming question is a marriage proposal and that Prufrock is afraid of these women, which is why he never utters the question. Yet lines 62-72 suggest that a very different kind of question is on Prufrock's mind. For one thing, Prufrock had known these women.

> And I have known the arms already, known them all—
> Arms that are bracelted and white and bare
> (But in the lamplight, downed with light brown hair!)
> Is it perfume from a dress
> That makes me so digress?
> Arms that lie along a table, or wrap about a shawl.
> > And should I then presume?
> > And how should I begin?

In the next stanza Prufrock provides us with an answer, the answer. The place where he should begin is the truth about himself. The overwhelming question he did not ask was not about a marriage proposal or a date or anything having to do with love. It was whether or not he should reveal to these women his true self.

> Shall I say, I have gone at dusk through narrow streets 70
> And watched the smoke that rises from the pipes
> Of lonely men in shirt-sleeves, leaning out of windows?...

This image of a lonely man is an image of life that is very different from the life Prufrock projected (or wished to project) when he was enjoying the company of those women in the lamplight with their hair down. When Prufrock visited these women he was dressed to the nines. He wore a "morning coat,[his] collar mounting firmly to the chin,/[His] necktie rich and modest, but asserted by a simple pin—" (lines 42-43). So what then is the relationship between this image of a well-dressed perhaps wealthy Prufrock and the world Prufrock would hide from these women? Prufrock could certainly be a wealthy interloper who only journeyed through the narrow streets where lonely men are leaning out of windows to visit these women of a different class. But I think the reverse is true. I think Prufrock is a man from the narrow streets, "a lonely man in shirtsleeves," who dresses in the costume of the wealthy so he can spend time with these women.

Furthermore, I think it does not matter if the women are of the same wealthy class as the image Prufrock is here projecting, or if they are from the same narrow streets that Prufrock seems to reject. What matters is that Prufrock does not want to reveal the truth about himself. And this, by the way, is why he is Hell. It is pretty much the same reason why Dante placed Guido in Hell; to whit, Guido abandoned his true self by becoming a monk; Prufrock abandoned his true self by keeping quiet about who he really was.

So the overwhelming question is not a question he would ask of the women; it is a question he asks of himself.

Thus, when Prufrock says "I should have been a pair of ragged claws/Scuttling across the floors of silent seas," he wants the pilgrim to know (for he is talking to the pilgrim here) that he wishes circumstances had been such that he wouldn't ponder the need to reveal his true self, that there had been no cause to speak about himself. Thus a "pair of ragged claws," an animal without a voice, living in the "silent seas," a place where no voice carries. Because then he wouldn't have been asked to reveal his true self to anyone. There would have been no question to ask, and he wouldn't be existing in this Hell where he now finds himself.

A DIGRESSION ON DIFFERENCES BETWEEN THE FIRST DRAFT OF PRUFROCK AND ITS FINAL FORM AS IT RELATES TO BOTH THE OVERWHELMING QUESTION AND THE CHARACTER OF PRUFROCK:

In the original draft of the poem, the section where Prufrock ponders the specific truth he might reveal to the women is longer by 38 lines. Here are the lines that Eliot cut placed within the five lines that remain in the final version of the poem.

> Shall I say, I have gone at dusk through
>   narrow streets   70
> And watched the smoke that rises from the
>   pipes
> Of lonely men in shirtsleeves, leaning out of
>   windows.

> [the following was cut]

> And when the evening woke and stared into its
>   blindness
> I heard the children whimpering in corners
> Where women took the air, standing in entries
> Women, spilling out of corsets, stood in entries
> Where the draughty gas-jet flickered
> And the oil cloth curled up stairs.
> And when the evening fought itself awake
> And the world was peeling oranges and
>   reading evening papers
> And boys were smoking cigarettes, drifted
>   helplessly together

A Ghost Wandering Through a Memory

In the fan of light spread out by the drugstore
    on the corner
Then I have gone at night through narrow
    streets,
Where evil houses leaning all together
Pointed a ribald finger at me in the darkness
Whispering all together, chuckled at me in the
    darkness.
And when the midnight turned and writhed in
    fever
I tossed the blankets back, to watch the
    darkness
Crawling among the papers on the table
It leapt to the floor and made a sudden hiss
And darted stealthily across the wall
Flattened itself upon the ceiling overhead
Stretched out its tentacles, prepared to leap
And when the dawn at length had realized
    itself
And turned with a sense of nausea, to see what
    it had stirred:
The eyes and feet of men -
I fumbled to the window to experience the
    world
And to hear my Madness singing, sitting on
    the kerbstone
[A blind old drunken man who sings and
    mutters,
With broken boot heels stained in many
    gutters]
And as he sang the world began to fall apart...

[lines that are in the final poem]

I should have been a pair of ragged claws
Scuttling across the floors of silent seas ...

[the following 4 lines were also cut]

I have seen the darkness creep along the wall
I have heard my Madness chatter before day
I have seen the world roll up into a ball
Then suddenly dissolve and fall away.

The 38 lines that make up the deleted passage are in fact an expanded version of the truth that Prufrock did not wish to share with the women at the tea party. The picture of life contained in these lines is in fact much more damning because it suggests that the Prufrock pictured here is on the verge of descending, like Hamlet, into madness. The world he would hide from the women at the tea party, his world, is here a world of evil houses, a world where the women were spilling out of their corsets, a world of darkness. So does this imagining of Prufrock's world change the nature of his interactions with the women at the tea party? I think not. If the women at the tea party were part of Prufrock's world, then not sharing his true self with them means he doesn't want them to know about how he feels about this world. He seems to feel sickened by it. If the women at the tea party are of a different class, then he simply doesn't want them to see that he is of a different class.

Why did Eliot cut these lines? Partly, I think, because the first three lines of the passage, the lines that made the final version of the poem, say all that Eliot wishes to say about the nature of the truth, the place where Prufrock should or could begin.

> Shall I say, I have gone at dusk through narrow streets   70
> And watched the smoke that rises from the pipes
> Of lonely men in shirtsleeves, leaning out of windows.

In other words, the lines that Eliot cut here were simply overkill. But the deleted lines do, I think, indicate that Prufrock, as a character, was cut from a different cloth than the typical Jamesian characters that some say inspired Eliot. And again, I do not imagine Eliot cut the lines so he could reshape Prufrock as a Jamesian type character; I think he cut the lines because the three he kept implied all the rest. The extra 38 would have simply unbalanced the poem itself – the more optimistic meaning (in my reading) at the end would have been lost as a result.

Finally, it is worth noting that the original subtitle of the poem was "Prufrock's Pervigilium"

(Prufrock's vigil). It is a subtitle that suggests that Prufrock is or was concerned about his soul and recalls the lines in the final poem in which he says "I have wept and prayed." Why did Eliot change the title? For the same reason that he cut the 38 lines describing the nature of the world that reveals Prufrock's true self. Eliot wanted to strike the right balance between the Prufrock who was concerned with the fate of his soul and the more optimistic, self-deprecating Prufrock we see near the end of the poem, once he has accepted his fate.

BACK TO THE UNFOLDING SCENE ONE MORE TIME

Once Prufrock establishes the fact that he would rather not reveal his true self (line 74), the focus of the poem shifts yet again.

We are approaching the moment of the taking of a tea. **BUT NOT YET**. The unfolding scene has been manipulated to a great degree until we have arrived at this point. Time and space have been manipulated. Our own thoughts about what is transpiring (or what has transpired) have also been manipulated. We are now ready both intellectually and emotionally for the end.

Prufrock and the pilgrim are perhaps stretched out on the floor. Prufrock raises in an offhand way the question of whether or not he might interject himself into the moment that has passed but which is about to appear on the movie screen of our imagination. But he seems less passionate than before about trying to impact what has already occurred. He is not afraid of the moment. He is too full of "tea and cakes and ices."

> And the afternoon, the evening, sleeps so peacefully! 75
> Smoothed by long fingers,
> Asleep ... tired ... or it malingers,
> Stretched on the floor, here beside you and me.
> Should I, after tea and cakes and ices,
> Have the strength to force the moment to its crisis? 80

And then he is past the moment (which I guess means that the tea and cakes and ices have been consumed). We, meaning Prufrock and the reader/pilgrim, are back in the present. The unfolding movie is **PAUSED** once again. One can imagine Prufrock glancing at the reader, shaking his head and pointing at the frozen moment before as he says the following lines:

> But though I have wept and fasted, wept and prayed,
> Though I have seen my head (grown slightly bald) brought in upon a platter,
> I am no prophet—and here's no great matter;

When did he weep and fast and pray? Is when

important? And why? So he can ask the question? Or so he can accept his fate (judgement)? It is the latter. And because he is mentioning this to the pilgrim in the present while the movie of his past has been paused, it seems reasonable to conclude that the weeping and the praying occurred after the movie of his life (which is in fact what we are watching) has concluded. Prufrock has been constantly wrestling with the overwhelming question (by weeping and praying) in this afterlife.

And what of the reference to John the Baptist? The Baptist wept and prayed and fasted to shine a light on the "truth" of Christ. Prufrock is similarly engaged in a struggle to shine a light on the truth of his actions for the pilgrim (an irony, surely, since the truth of his actions was to keep a truth hidden). But he also acknowledges here that this truth is a small truth; he is no prophet (like John the Baptist) with a great truth. It is also worth noting that there is no sense of despair here; the tone of his self-deprecating comment about his baldness certainly seems the opposite of despair. What one can say here about Prufrock is that he has not only begun to accept this fate, he has begun to accept everything about who he once was (at least until the next time he thinks about the journey and the overwhelming question and the scene begins to unfold once again.).

Then Prufrock shares how he felt when he died. It is a moment of absolute honesty (would that he had been so honest in sharing his true self with those women).

> I have seen the moment of my greatness
> > flicker,
> And I have seen the eternal Footman hold my
> > coat, and snicker,   **85**
> And in short, I was afraid.

He has seen his life vanish ("the moment of his greatness") – He has seen death and was afraid, and who wouldn't have been afraid at the moment Death arrives. But the implication here is that he is no longer afraid, like Guido Montefelatro from Dante's *Inferno*.

WOULD ACTING DIFFERENTLY HAVE MATTERED?:

One could imagine that the poem might end with Prufrock's memory of his death, but Prufrock himself is not quite ready to give up the ghost. For one thing, he wants to explore the possibility that if he had in fact acted differently, if he had revealed his true self to the women at the tea party, then perhaps life would have been different.

The next stanza (lines 87-95) provides an imaginative examination of what might have happened. And yet he is also talking to the pilgrim as he imagines this possibility. In other words, once again Prufrock is engaging the memory as if he could impact the past in the here and now of the present. He is squeezing two different moments in time into a single moment, an action underscored by the very fact that he is also pondering the effect of squeezing "the universe into a ball."

> And would it have been worth it, after all,
> After the cups, the marmalade, the tea,
> Among the porcelain, among some talk of you and me,
> Would it have been worthwhile, 90
> To have bitten off the matter with a smile,
> To have squeezed the universe into a ball
> To roll it toward some overwhelming question,
> To say: "I am Lazarus, come from the dead,
> Come back to tell you all, I shall tell you all" — 95

In this conflated moment, he comes up with a question he might ask in his present condition as a denizen of Hell. What if he were able to insert himself into the past and say to those women "I am Lazarus, come from the dead,/Come back to tell you all, I shall tell you all." This is an interesting line for a number of reasons. Which Lazarus is Eliot/Prufrock referring to? Is this an allusion to the Lazarus Jesus raised from the dead? If so, then Prufrock is actively inviting us to imagine the possibility that he could return from his present place in Hell to impact the path. Is Prufrock/Eliot alluding to the parable of the rich man and Lazarus (a different Lazarus who was sent

A Ghost Wandering Through a Memory

to Heaven, while the rich man was sent to Hell, unable to return)? In this second parable, the rich man looked up to heaven and asked Abraham to send Lazarus back to earth to warn his brothers about the wages of sin. Abraham refused; no one went back to earth to tell anyone anything. If Prufrock/Eliot is alluding to this parable, then are we meant to understand that Prufrock must remain in Hell, just as Guido must remain in Hell?

I think Eliot is referring to both. We are meant to imagine the possibility that Prufrock could impact the past, at least in his imagination. And we are meant to acknowledge that he cannot impact the past as a point of fact, for he is Hell. Of course as far as the action of the poem is concerned, the question that Prufrock is asking is: would such a claim have made it worthwhile if the women didn't really respond to it. So Prufrock imagines what he might have said, and then he imagines that the women do not respond.

> If one, settling a pillow by her head,
>> Should say: "That is not what I meant at all;
>> That is not it, at all."

To make sense of the response of the women (lines 97-98), we need to reflect on the gap between what know from the poem about Prufrock's relationship with these women and what that relationship implies. We know from earlier in the poem that Prufrock is on intimate terms with these women (lines 62-67). These lines are perhaps the most significant lines in the poem, so I will quote them a third time:

> And I have known the arms already, known them all—
> Arms that are braceleted and white and bare
> (But in the lamplight, downed with light brown hair!)
> Is it perfume from a dress
> That makes me so digress?
> Arms that lie along a table, or wrap about a shawl.
> > And should I then presume?
> > And how should I begin?

Once can certainly imagine here (an implication) that from moment to moment, these women might want something more from Prufrock, greater attention, flattery, extended kisses.

One can also imagine that Prufrock, thinking perhaps that now was the time to reveal the truth about who he really was (a lonely man in shirt sleeves), might during the tea party offer up something the women were not expecting and did not really want.

Such as the claim that he was Lazarus returned from the dead.

Or an indication of who he really was.

One can then imagine that to such a claim or statement, they would respond as Prufrock imagines they might respond.

>   If one, settling a pillow [which suggests a very
>   intimate tea party] by her head,
>   Should say: "That is not what I meant at all;
>   That is not it, at all."

But Prufrock does not address the worthiness
of the first scenario and goes on immediately
in the next stanza to suggest a new but similar
scenario.

>   And would it have been worth it, after all,
>   Would it have been worthwhile,   100
>   After the sunsets and the dooryards and the
>   sprinkled streets,
>   After the novels, after the teacups, after the
>   skirts that trail along the floor—
>   And this, and so much more?—
>   It is impossible to say just what I mean!
>   But as if a magic lantern threw the nerves in
>   patterns on a screen: 105
>   Would it have been worth while
>   If one, settling a pillow or throwing off a
>   shawl,
>   And turning toward the window, should say:
>   "That is not it at all,
>   That is not what I meant, at all.   110

The major difference between the two scenarios
is that in the second scenario, Prufrock does not
tell us what claim he makes; he tells us in fact

that it is impossible to explain to the reader/
pilgrim what he means, just that he imagines that
whatever he wanted to have happened would
have done so magically, without his directly doing
anything, which makes sense given that he never
raised the overwhelming question anyway. The
smaller question he ponders here is would he have
been satisfied with the outcome in this vague,
anything-can-happen context, if someone again
said: "this is not what I meant." And the answer is
no.

{Notes: 1) The "magic lantern" that "threw the
nerves in patterns on a screen" (line 105) deserves
some discussion. Magic lanterns per se had been
around since the mid-1600s and reached their
zenith in the late 19th century. But the images a
magic lantern might project are little more than
shadows. I think Eliot was thinking of a movie
projector projecting the images of what Prufrock
imagines might have happened with the women.
(See #2 below for a comment on Eliot's love of
the cinema.) Thus the phrase "the nerves" likely
refers to what is/was happening in Prufrock's
brain vis-à-vis the memory of what led up to the
overwhelming question; and these images, which
are in fact a detailed "pattern" of light and dark,
are projected onto a movie screen. In other words,
what Prufrock imagines seems true, it has the

feeling of reality, but it is without substance; it is a flickering, false reality.

2) David Trotter, in his essay titled "T. S. Eliot and the Cinema" (*Modernism/modernity*, Volume 13, Number 2, April 2006, pp. 237-265), asserts that Eliot possessed an "enduring preoccupation" with the cinema. Moreover, Trotter asserts that Eliot's poetry as a whole is often structured more like film with cuts and pans and close-ups, and so each poem becomes a montage of scenes. I believe we see the first evidence of this approach in "Prufrock." 3) In 1910, there were 7,000 theaters showing movies in the United States. According to *The Ottawa Herald*, February, 1910, on any given Sunday in New York City alone, 500,000 people watched movies in 300 theaters. So it seems plausible to say the least that Eliot would make an allusion to the movies in a poem which in some respects is a reflection on the illusory nature of reality. This reading of line 105 also gives greater meaning to line 84: "I have seen the moment of my greatness flicker" when Prufrock was recalling the moment of his actual death, for the word "flicker" suggests that Eliot is drawing a parallel between the life of a person and the movie of that life, a parallel that lies at the foundation of my reading of this poem as essentially being in part a "cinematic" presentation of a pivotal moment in Prufrock's life.]

Again, most critics suggest that the women are responding to a marriage proposal from Prufrock by saying they have been misunderstood, which is an awful way to be rejected. This line of reasoning generally begins with an assessment of the kind of character Prufrock was, the assertion that he is a timid Jamesian type, and ends using this character assessment as a way of determining the nature of the question. But this kind of reasoning seems backwards to me. The poem itself gives us clues as to what the nature of the question is (see the discussion of the *Hamlet* stanza below). And the nature of the question gives us clues as to the kind of character Prufrock actually is (or was). Moreover, the response of the women could have been dictated by any number of plausible questions or claims. The question could just as easily have been "Do you see who I truly am?" and the indifference of the response would have been just as awful. But it is in the very next stanza, the Hamlet stanza, that my suspicion that the overwhelming question has to do with revealing one's true identity is confirmed.

THE MEANING OF THE *HAMLET* STANZA:

The Hamlet stanza refocuses our understanding on what the overwhelming question deals with. It is in part an existential question.

> No! I am not Prince Hamlet, nor was meant to
>   be;
> Am an attendant lord, one that will do
> To swell a progress, start a scene or two,
> Advise the prince; no doubt, an easy tool,
> Deferential, glad to be of use,   115
> Politic, cautious, and meticulous;
> Full of high sentence, but a bit obtuse;
> At times, indeed, almost ridiculous—
> Almost, at times, the Fool.

In response to the question of would Prufrock have been satisfied if he had pushed his claims or questions on the women at the tea party, Prufrock delivers a resounding "No!" it would not have been worthwhile. The rest of the Hamlet stanza offers insight into why he thinks this. Line 111 is significant. Prufrock suggests he was not meant to consider existential questions such as Hamlet pondered. But consider here the irony of the half line "nor was meant to be" which is both a reference to his fate (he died and is now a ghost, so he was not "meant to be"), and a reference to the kind of existential question Hamlet considered and which Prufrock, in spite of his claim to the contrary, has been considering throughout the whole poem (and here it is Eliot himself who confirms this because as we read line 111, we hear in our minds: "I am not Prince Hamlet, nor was meant to be *or not to be That is the question!*). Thus, Prufrock, like Hamlet is wrestling with an existential question, and the result of that wrestling, is that Prufrock, like Hamlet, hides his true self. *"To be [my true self] or not to be [my true self], that is the question."*

Then in lines 112-119, Prufrock says that rather than Hamlet, he is more like Polonius, a blustering old fool. And yet here too both Eliot and Prufrock are telling us about the nature of the overwhelming question Prufrock has been thinking of. What do I mean here? Simply this: the most important piece of advice that Polonius gives to his son Laertes is "to thine ownself be true." So the allusion to Polonius reminds us (reader/pilgrim) that the overwhelming question Prufrock has been struggling with is about revealing one's true identity.

That these allusions, which seem to bookend the concept of revealing one's true identity, and the *revealed* meaning of the poem dovetail at this the climax of the poem seems proof enough that Prufrock is concerned with the fact that he never let those women know his true self.

[Note: Ezra Pound wanted to cut the *Hamlet* stanza, but Eliot was adamant that the lines remain in the poem. In other words, Pound did not grasp the full meaning of the poem.]

A Ghost Wandering Through a Memory

THE LAST FEW SCENES OF THE MOVIE OF PRUFROCK'S LIFE AND THE END OF THE POEM:

Once we understand that the overwhelming question is about revealing one's true identity, once this is made clear for all to see, Prufrock wraps up his journey/tale rather quickly. First, as in *Hamlet*, the play within a play is concluded. And then the larger play containing the smaller play concludes and we can go home (until Prufrock takes the stage again and we as pilgrim return).

Both Prufrock and the pilgrim/reader look at the extended scene of Prufrock's life. In fact Prufrock fast forwards to the end. He says:

> I grow old ... I grow old ... 120
> I shall wear the bottoms of my trousers rolled.
>
> Shall I part my hair behind? Do I dare to eat a peach?
> I shall wear white flannel trousers, and walk upon the beach.

The questions here are somewhat superfluous because the real questions have already been put to rest. The image of an old man walking on a beach with his trousers rolled up is what you might expect of many an old man. Also note how in old age, Prufrock's abilty to "dare" has been reduced to pondering whether or not to eat a peach, a far cry from daring to disturb the

Universe at the beginning of the tale (line 45), perhaps because his teeth were no longer up to the challenge.

Then the movie is over (the play within the play). You can imagine Prufrock and the pilgrim/reader turning from the blank screen and Prufrock confiding to the pilgrim:

> I have heard the mermaids singing, each to each.

Why mermaids? Mermaids sit at the intersection of the mythic and the real. They are the gatekeepers, if you will, to all of the imaginary or supernatural realms that are generally beyond mortal experience. In this instance, they serve to demarcate the line between the real and the mythic, just as they are also an indication of Prufrock's journey from one realm to the other. Are the mermaids also symbolic reflections of the women from earlier in the poem? Perhaps. The women from earlier talk of Michelangelo, but we do not hear their words. The mermaids sing to each other, but we do not hear their songs. And Prufrock (and we, the pilgrim) have lingered with both. In the final analysis, however, it does not matter if one group properly mirrors the other. The women from earlier point us in the direction of the question Prufrock must face. And the mermaids point us in the direction of where Prufrock now must exist as a result of trying to hide from the truth that is/was revealed by that

A Ghost Wandering Through a Memory

question.

Then in an almost jovial tone (not sad, his story is over, so why wouldn't he be somewhat happy, at least satisfied, even content, he has come to terms with his fate, at least for the moment), perhaps he is even clapping the pilgrim on the back as they head back to where they began:

> I do not think that they will sing to me.   125

Because he is already dead – mermaids prey upon the living.

And then in a tone that might seem to the pilgrim to be the tone of a madman, for it certainly seems over the top, but which might also be characterized as a reignited passion for living. Still, I have a hard time thinking Eliot is one-hundred percent serious here. It is almost like Eliot suddenly began to channel Tennyson in lines 126-128. Maybe this is a tongue-in-cheek nod to the Romantics.

> I have seen them riding seaward on the waves
> Combing the white hair of the waves blown back
> When the wind blows the water white and black.

And then Prufrock is speaking directly to the "you," the pilgrim from the beginning. I can imagine Prufrock speaking these lines to the pilgrim with a lively, slightly exaggerated tone, as if the two had just left a pub. I am certain of the tongue-in-cheek tone

> We have lingered in the chambers of the sea
> By sea-girls wreathed with seaweed red and brown 130
> Till human voices wake us, and we drown.

    Prufrock is, of course, commenting on the journey they have taken and how they are now essentially back where they began, a place outside of both time and space, a magical place of the imagination, of consciousness, a primordial place, a place where ragged claws scuttle across the bottom of the ocean, animals without voices, a voiceless place of silent seas, this is where they have lingered while Prufrock shared his tale. The surreal, playful, fantastical quality of the ending sequence also reminds me of the films of Georges Méliès, the French symbolist artist turned movie director (*The Astronomer's Dream*, 1898; *The Magic Lantern*, 1903; *The Eclipse: or the Courtship of the Sun and Moon*, 1907; to name three).

    Once Prufrock's tale is over, the world can intrude ("till human voices wake us") and Prufrock (and the pilgrim) must die yet again. And yet since both Prufrock and the pilgrim/reader exist outside of time, and since death is something that will occur over and over in their dual memory, death itself is not something to be afraid of or even sad about. Indeed, the death of Prufrock here seems both staged and ritualized; moreover, it is a ritual that occurs every time Prufrock tells a pilgrim his tale.

A few critics have commented on the ritual nature of the end. Critic Ron Banerjee states at the end of an essay titled "The Dantean Overview: The Epigraph to Prufrock" (Vol. 87, No. 7, *Comparative Literature* (Dec., 1972), pp. 962-966) that "The shift to the present tense in 'wake' and 'drown' in the last movement, makes both the illusion of escape and awakening, which is tantamount to death, habitual and therefore mechanical. It not only throws the poem back to the opening drawing room scene, but by suggesting a closed cyclical structure, turns Prufrock into someone akin to the marionette-liked damned, who eternally reiterate their gestures in the *Inferno*."

The insight here is significant, for Banerjee is commenting both on the ritualized nature of the telling of Prufrock's tale, and the eternal nature of Prufrock's condition in the telling of that tale. But Banerjee has not gone quite far enough. Not only is Prufrock like the damned in Dante's *Inferno*, he plays the exact same role in "Prufrock" (the poem). He is of the damned. In other words, like Guido, he is dead, even though we can say with some measured irony that he is of the undead.

Of course, this reading of the end begs one final question. How does the title of the poem square with this reading? How is this a love song? Well, in fact, the title is ironic. It is not a love song to a specific woman, or to women in general. It is not even a love song to love. It is a love song to life itself, for now that Prufrock is no longer among the living, all he can do is wish that he were and remember how different his life might have been if he had embraced that life. So he embraces this tale with passion, a self-deprecating wit that appears from time to time, and a tongue-in-cheek vitality, especially in the end, that he did not quite possess when he was alive.

Let me just add that this was the first poem Eliot had published as a professional poet. It is not modernist, as most critics assert, though it anticipates modernism. So too, the poem is not an interior monologue solely, for in a dramatic sense the pilgrim is always on stage with Prufrock. The poem does possess certain symbolist qualities, rather like Baudelaire, and so I think harkens back to an earlier age rather than anticipating the kind of modernism that explodes with Joyce. But this is to be expected. Eliot was 27 when the poem was published. He was still experimenting with form. Perhaps this is also why he seems to bring elements of the cinema into his poem as well.

So what I think happened is this. Eliot writes a great poem partially influenced by the French symbolist poets, partially influenced by the mysticism of Yeats, the spiritual power of

Tennyson, partly influenced by the emerging technology of the cinema and the early cinema itself. Ezra Pound loves the poem and helps him get the poem published.

The poem is published to great acclaim, but from the beginning it is misread (even Pound misreads it, for why else would he have wished to cut the *Hamlet* stanza from the poem). Everyone seems to view Prufrock as alive. Eliot just takes this in. He accepts the judgement of his readers. He accepts the judgment of Pound and pursues this new form with more vigor. He and Pound work on "The Wasteland" together as an apprentice might work with his master. Modernist poetry is born.

Something like that.

Peter Damian Bellis is the author of numerous articles and non-fiction books as well as One Last Dance with Lawrence Welk & Other Stories (1996, River Boat Books), which was a 1997 Minnesota Book Award Finalist, and also The Conjure Man (2010, River Boat Books), which made the informal (and therefore unpublicized), long list for The National Book Award. (The author has the letter from one of the fiction judges for 2010 that informed of him his book's fate and will produce this letter to any who ask to see it.) He taught writing and literature at Pennsylvania College of Technology, Williamsport, Pennsylvania from August 2008 until December 2018. His latest novel, Gods Among Gazelles, was published in 2020.

Made in the USA
Columbia, SC
16 February 2025